The Quotable Wine Lover

The Quotable Wine Lover

EDITED BY
KATE FIDUCCIA

Main Street
A division of Sterling Publishing Co., Inc.
New York

Library of Congress Cataloging-in-Publication Data available

10   9   8   7   6   5   4   3   2   1

Published by Main Street, a division of Sterling Publishing Co., Inc.
387 Park Avenue South, New York, NY 10016

© 2000 by Kate Fiduccia
This edition published by Sterling Publishing in 2004

Distributed in Canada by Sterling Publishing
c/o Canadian Manda Group, 165 Dufferin Street
Toronto, Ontario, Canada M6K 3H6
Distributed in Great Britain by Chrysalis Books Group PLC
The Chrysalis Building, Bramley Road, London W10 6SP, England
Distributed in Australia by Capricorn Link (Australia) Pty. Ltd.
P.O. Box 704, Windsor, NSW 2756, Australia

Sterling ISBN 1-4027-1647-8

For when the wine is in, the wit is out.

—Thomas Becon

Table of Contents

Foreword

The cool Provençal morning air was better than a cup of coffee, which is what I would normally have at six in the morning. I was perched on the back of a tractor driven by Maurice, a Provençal "paysan," winding through the narrow streets of a thirteenth-century village with a population of less than three hundred. It didn't take long to reach the village limit. Soon we were heading through cherry and peach groves, olive orchards, and wild brush.

I'll never forget that smell. After about twenty minutes we penetrated a wall of plane trees and settled in a vineyard to begin our task of attaching the loose vine branches to metal wires and snipping off others. This process helps control the vine growth and prepares the vineyard for the ensuing harvest. Maurice instructed me on how to cut and tie and we worked for about three hours. I was now awake but couldn't understand how we could possibly keep up this pace until nightfall. Maurice called for a break, a "casse-croute," or "break the crust." We settled under a tree and he pulled from his sack a large country loaf of bread, a dry sausage, and a bottle of wine. I was expected something like a croissant or a pain au chocolat. But no, this was a farmers snack! After a few bites and a glass (or two) of "vin ordinaire" I asked if I could extend my break a bit longer.

I was in the heart of Provence spending a year studying French language and literature. What I came back with more than anything else was French culture. Especially wine culture. My life in Provence eventually lead me to other adventures throughout France in the world of food and wine—as an apprentice in the kitchen of a two-star Michelin restaurant in Paris, an assistant on a duck farm specializing in foie gras and duck products, and as a cook in a country restaurant in the Armagnac region. In every new adventure, the vineyards were within reach, and at every opportunity I would escape to visit the wineries and talk with the winemakers. Their stories—full of passion and history—helped me understand wine in a much more organic way than had I learned about it in a classroom.

After four years in the French vineyards and culinary temples I returned home to the United States. I knew wine was my calling, but it only made sense to me in the context of food. So after several years both as a waiter and training as a sommelier in New York's finest restaurants, I became the sommelier at Montrachet. Fortunately, my experiences in France allowed me to discuss wine with our clientele in a way that is more personal than technical. How could wine be reduced to a discussion of its alcoholic content and sulfites? Wine evokes much more than just a flavor; it brings back memories and experiences.

Now as the wine director at Montrachet and as an importer in search of special "discoveries" for our clientele and others, I travel to France on a regular basis. My import company, Jeroboam Wines, has allowed me to visit every major wine-producing region of France and I have seen wine consumed as a beverage at informal "casse-croutes" and at formal banquets. It is a common denominator, a unifying element that brings people together in a magical way. Ships are launched and treaties are signed with it. Breaking bread and sharing wine are the most symbolic acts of generosity and peace that I know of.

What is special and remarkable about THE QUOTABLE WINE LOVER is how—through hundreds of quotes from people of different ages and professions, of varying religious and political beliefs—a common voice comes through. This voice applauds the many facets of wine, and its significance to so many different people. Declarations from laypeople and professionals alike enable the reader to

learn about, and vicariously celebrate, the pleasures of wine.

—Daniel Johnnes
New York City
July 2000

Introduction

My own introduction to wine came during my seventeenth summer, when I was crowned the 1979 North American Grape Stomping Queen at Hudson Valley Wine Co. in New York. The afternoon with my parents was a beautiful sunny day that began with a tour of the historic winery in the morning. After a delicious picnic lunch on their expansive grounds overlooking the Hudson River, the emcee on the outdoor stage announced the grape-stomping competition would begin shortly. What the heck? I thought, so I gave it a try. I laughed as I vigorously squished cratefuls of grapes between my toes while keeping time with the live band's rock n' roll music. The finals were tougher than I thought. My competition was two female cadets from West Point! The juice gods—and Bacchus (who must have given me preference for my four years of Latin)—shined on me and let the grapes' liquid pour forth to victory! Even veteran reporter Lloyd Dobbins reported my triumph on a New York affiliate news station that same evening.

My love of wine and food lead me to an invaluable education at Cornell University's Hotel School where I majored in Food and Beverage Management. As with most other hotel school students and thousands of other Cornellians, "Wine & Spirits" was one of the favorite classes on campus. Each Friday afternoon, we tasted wines from across the globe and gleaned knowledge from the best instructors and guest lecturers from the wine industry. I was able to put this good knowledge to use later on when my husband and I bought our own Italian restaurant. Featuring local wines from southern New York, our wine list was comprehensive and we personally shared many special wine moments together with our customers and friends.

While winemaking and its lovers date back centuries throughout Europe, winemaking in America is relatively new. It wasn't until 1823 when John Adlum wrote the first book about American winegrowing (as opposed to the British North American colonies) with its assumptions that American wine was to be developed with the grape varieties native to the continent.

The quotes I've collected in this book are an expansive collection that span from the Bible to today's wine enthusiasts. From the Christian prophets and disciples to the prohibition of wine in the world's second largest religion, Islam, their stories include wine as a joyous part of celebrating life.

Words of wisdom ring so very true from those who have made wine their livelihood. Vintners, sommeliers, restaurateurs, and wine critics all share their views and love of wine. My hope is that you will enjoy these quotes from people who love or have loved wine. Salute!

K. F.

1

By the Glass or by the Bottle
Contemporary Wine Lovers

A person with increasing knowledge and sensory education may derive infinite enjoyment from wine.

ERNEST HEMINGWAY

———•••———

Never, never trust anyone who asks for white wine. It means they're phonies.

BETTE DAVIS

For some obscure reason, some authorities seem bent on making the drinking of wine a ritual more complicated than chess. They have succeeded in inhibiting a large section of the public and depriving them of one of the greatest pleasures known to man.

CRAIG CLAIBORNE

When it came to writing about wine, I did what almost everybody does—faked it.

ART BUCHWALD

For wine has participated universally in the cultural ascent of man, serving as a festive drink at his birth, a solemn drink at his death, a sacred drink in religious ceremonies, and a stimulant of discussion in symposium and intellectual colloquia.

SALVATORE P. LUCIA, MD,
PHYSICIAN AND WRITER

There must be always wine and fellowship or we are truly lost.

ANN FAIRBAIRN, WRITER

Wine, it's in my veins and I can't get it out.

BURGESS MEREDITH, ACTOR AND OENOPHILE

Great people talk about ideas, average people talk about things, and small people talk about wine.

FRAN LEBOWITZ

[They] face each other across the road . . . like mad old duchesses in party clothes.

HUGH JOHNSON, ON THE VINEYARDS OF
SOUTHWESTERN FRANCE

Bread and wine and thou—it's all there.

BARRY BENEPE, DIRECTOR, GREENMARKETS,
ON SELLING WINE AT FARMERS' MARKETS

Wine books flow from printing presses like water from broken spigots.

HOWARD GOLDBERG

To take wine into our mouths is to savor a droplet of the river of human history.

FROM THE HALLMARK GALLERY,
NEW YORK TIMES, MARCH 8, 1967

Wine has been a part of civilized life for some seven thousand years. It is the only beverage that feeds the body, soul and spirit of man and at the same time stimulates the mind . . .

ROBERT MONDAVI

———•◦•———

Three be the things I shall never attain: envy, content and sufficient champagne.

DOROTHY PARKER

Champagne is the one thing that gives me zest when I am tired.

BRIGITTE BARDOT

———❦———

I haven't had much luck in pairing red wine with lobster.

JASPER WHITE,
CHEF AND AUTHOR

Wine speaks to all the senses: the eyes behold the color, tone and shade; the nose, the bouquet; the fingers and lips caress the cool crystal; the ears delight in the subtle swishing of the liquid; the tongue rejoices in the reward of a rich harvest.

MARY LOU POSCH, WINE LOVER

———

Wine is made to be drunk as women are made to be loved; profit by the freshness of youth or the splendor of maturity; do not await decrepitude.

THEOPHILE MALVEZIN

Wine is the sort of alcoholic beverage that does not destroy but enriches life; does not distort but clarifies perspective; does not seduce except in a way worth humanly being seduced.

BILL ST. JOHN

Sip, Swirl, Swallow!

MICHELINE R. RAMOS, WINE LOVER

Whenever I drink champagne I either laugh or cry . . . I get so emotional! I love champagne.

TINA TURNER

Champagne, if you are seeking the truth, is better than a lie detector. It encourages a man to be expansive, even reckless, while lie detectors are only a challenge to tell lies successfully.

GRAHAM GREENE

It was such an exquisite 1964 Bordeaux that one sip was more like inhaling a soft fragrance than imbibing a liquid.

ELLEN ELLER, WINE LOVER

Wisdom doesn't automatically come with old age. Nothing does—except wrinkles. It's true, some wines improve with age. But only if the grapes were good in the first place.

ABIGAIL VAN BUREN

If your heart is warm with happiness, you'll need a glass—if sorrow chills your heart, have two!

HANNU, WINE LOVER

———•◦•◦•———

It is not a wine that commands your attention, but rather, rewards it.

DAVE GUIMOND, WINE LOVER

Appreciating old wine is like making love to a very old lady. It is possible. It can even be enjoyable. But it requires a bit of imagination.

ANDRE TCHELISTCHEFF

———•◦•◦•———

There are two reasons for drinking wine . . . when you are thirsty, to sure it; the other, when you are not thirsty, to prevent it . . . prevention is better than cure.

THOMAS LOVE PEACOCK, WINE LOVER

Wine is a living liquid containing no preservatives. Its life cycle comprises youth, maturity, old age and death. When not treated with reasonable respect it will wicken and die.

JULIA CHILD

And so the souls of men and their wine live for eternity with the grace of their God.

JAMES BIANCAMANO, WINE LOVER

To buy very good wine nowadays requires only money. To serve it to your guests is a sign of fatigue.

WILLIAM F. BUCKLEY

A bottle of wine begs to be shared; I have never met a miserly wine lover.

CLIFTON FADIMAN

After working late one night, I drank a bottle of frisky Beaujolais and slipped into bed beside my lady love. By moonlight I pursed my lips and into her ear whispered, "moelleux, moelleux." She bolted up, shouting, "What the hell is wrong with you?"

A. D. LIVINGSTON, AUTHOR OF *ON THE GRILL, STRICTLY STEAK*, AND OTHER COOKBOOKS

I made wine out of raisins so I wouldn't have to wait for it to age.

STEVEN WRIGHT

———•••———

I've always been impressed by Washington State merlot. It just sort of jumped out of the glass at me . . . You just feel this is right: this is not an attempt at something, this is something.

JANCIS ROBINSON M.W.

Eat bread at pleasure, drink wine by measure.

RANDLE COTGRAVE, WINE LOVER

———◆◆◆◆———

I'm like old wine. They don't bring me out very often, but I'm well preserved.

ROSE KENNEDY, FAMILY MATRIARCH, ON
HER 100TH BIRTHDAY IN 1991

You have only so many bottles in your life, never drink a bad one.

LEN EVANS, WINE LOVER

———•❖•———

[I]n France, drunkenness is a consequence, never an intention. A drink is felt as the spinning out of a pleasure, not as the necessary cause of an effect which is sought: wine is not only a philtre, it is also the leisurely act of drinking.

ROLAND BARTHES

[Sauvignon blanc] bangs you in the mouth—like an old peasant with his wooden shoe . . . The Sauvignon is the whipper-snapper. It's not solid enough. It's violent, it's sharp, it bites, it cries, it's like a ferocious dog you keep on a leash.

TROISGROS, AS QUOTED BY
ISRAEL SHENKER IN THE *NEW YORK TIMES*

Now wines are wonders; great wines are magical; and winemakers are mad. Like horse fanciers, they are always trying to improve the breed.

WILLIAM E. MASSEE

I love the vocabulary of wine. It's a sumptuous feeling to roll those gorgeous words around your mouth as though you were tasting a Cote-Rotie. There's *remuage* and *vendage* for the back palate, and *pourriture* for the tip of the tongue. For a really silky little word try *moelleux*. Linger on it, purse your lips on that opening syllable, and say it to someone you wish to seduce.

When it's a few guys quaffing something darkly tannic shout out *gout de terrior*—make it butch, make it gruff. I like to say the word *crus* and really get that 'r' ringing round the epiglottis—good for clearing chesty colds.

And for the sheer bravado, the thrilling virtuosity of it just unroll *trockenbeerenauslese* in the shower first thing in the morning. Nothing like it to get you pumped.

MICHAEL STEPHENSON, CO-AUTHOR WITH DANIEL JOHNNES OF *DANIEL JOHNNES'S TOP 200 WINES*

A good wine is like a gentle kiss, its effect throughout the meal is scintillatingly sensual in an elegantly understated way.

FRANCES TABEEK, WINE ENTHUSIAST

———•••———

The depth of experience fine wine can bring to a dinner, particularly [a bottle] that has been through the past 100 years, makes you take stock of your own life.

NEIL DEGRASSE TYSON, WINE COLLECTOR AND DIRECTOR OF HAYDEN PLANETARIUM

I like sweet wines. My idea has always been that when you're young, you like sweet wines; and then you get sophisticated, and you drink dry white; and then you get knowledgeable, and you drink heavy reds; and then you get old, and you drink sweet again.

SALLY JESSY RAPHAEL, WINE COLLECTOR AND ENTHUSIAST

I don't go by the ratings. I buy wine that tastes good. Statistically, anybody's ability to predict what will be a good wine a decade from now is limited.

RICHARD THALER, BEHAVIORAL ECONOMIST AND AUTHOR

At least once a day you should do something purely
for enjoyment, and wine is my way of relaxing.

YOUNG UCK KIM, PROFESSIONAL
VIOLINIST AND WINE COLLECTOR

Red wine is a great accompaniment to meat.

MARIO LEMIEUX, RETIRED PROFESSIONAL
HOCKEY PLAYER AND WINE COLLECTOR

Drinking wine is just a part of life, like eating food.

FRANCIS FORD COPPOLA, MOVIEMAKER AND WINE COLLECTOR

———————

Wine is a living thing. It is made, not only of grapes and yeasts, but of skill and patience. When drinking it remember that to the making of that wine has gone, not only the labor and care of years, but the experience of centuries.

ALLAN SICHEL

It is not the year, the producer, or even the label that determines the quality of the wine; it is the wine in the glass, whatever the label or producer or year . . . Drink wine, not labels.

Dr. Maynard Amerine

———

Drinking good wine with good food in good company is one of life's most civilized pleasures.

Michael Broadbent

I cook with wine; sometimes I even add it to the food.

W.C. FIELDS

———————

The wine seems to be very closed-in and seems to have entered a dumb stage. Sort of a Marcel Meursault.

PAUL S. WINALSKI

Wine—it should be enjoyed for the benefits of the soul—and nothing more.

PETER FIDUCCIA, WINE LOVER

Δ

[P]eople are always pointing fingers about wine not being good for the diet. But great wine and great food are two of the few pleasures we have left.

JIM DAVIS, CARTOONIST AND
CREATOR OF GARFIELD

2

No Wine Before Its Time
Wine in History

[There is] a great abundance [of vines] in many parts . . . Of these hedge grapes we made neere twentie gallons of wine, which was like our British wine, but certainly they would prove good were they well manured.

CAPTAIN JOHN SMITH, IN PRECOLONIAL VIRGINIA, REPORTING ON THE TASTE OF ONE OF THE FIRST BATCHES OF AMERICAN WINE.

There are things whose value depends upon only their rarity, such as . . . exquisite wines. Since we can only procure things from particular territories of very small scale, it follows that their quantity be very limited: no amount of hard work is able to increase their quantity.

RICARDO, ENGLISH ECONOMIST

[M]ethods for storing wine once it has been harvested differ greatly depending on the climate. In the Alps it is put into hooped barrels and in the depths of winter, fires are lit to prevent it from freezing.

PLINY THE ELDER, ON WINE STORAGE

Wine can be considered with good reason as the most healthful and hygienic of all beverages.

LOUIS PASTEUR

Wine drinkers never make artists.

GRATINOS

Your stomach is your wine cellar, keep the stock small and cool.

CHARLES TOVEY

The wine in the bottle does not quench thirst.

GEORGE HERBERT

The Spanish wine, my God, it is foul, catpiss is champagne compared, this is the sulphurous urination of some aged horse.

D. H. LAWRENCE

Alanso of Aragon was wont to say in commendation of age, that "age appears to be best in four things—old wood best to burn, old wine to drink, old friends to trust, and old authors to read."

FRANCIS BACON

——•◦•——

He who aspires to be a serious wine drinker must drink claret.

SAMUEL JOHNSON

What though youth gave love and roses age still leaves us friends and wine.

THOMAS MOORE

⸺⸱⸱⸱⸱⸺

Wine rejoices the heart of man and joy is the mother of all virtues.

JOHANN WOLFGANG VON GOETHE

Nothing makes the future look so rosy as to contemplate it through a glass of Chambertin.

NAPOLEON BONAPARTE

———◆◆◆———

I like best the wine drunk at the cost of others.

DIOGENES THE CYNIC

Quickly, bring me a beaker of wine, so that I may wet my mind and say something clever.

ARISTOPHANES

———•◦•———

Drink wine and have the gout; drink none and have it too.

COGAN, HAVEN OF HEALTH

Never spare the parson's wine nor the baker's pudding.

BENJAMIN FRANKLIN,
POOR RICHARD'S ALMANAC

———◦⟡◦———

Then the next health to friends of mine
Loving the brave Burgundian Wine.

HERRICK'S *HESPERIDES*

Nothing more excellent or valuable than wine was ever granted by the gods to man.

PLATO

———•◦•———

Bronze is the mirror of the form; wine, of the heart.

AESCHYLUS

The vine bears three kinds of grapes: the first of pleasure, the next of intoxication, and the third of disgust.

ANARCHIS

———◦•◦•◦———

Wine, to a gifted bard, is a
Mount that merrily races;
From watered wits,
No good has ever grown.

CRATINUS

Wine makes a man more pleased with himself, I do not say that it makes him more pleasing to others.

SAMUEL JOHNSON

———

Wine is like rain: when it falls on the mire it but makes it fouler, but when it strikes the good soil wakes it to beauty and bloom.

JOHN MAY

In vino veritas—In wine there is truth.

PLINY THE ELDER

———◦◦———

If wine tells truth,—and so have said the wise,—
It makes me laugh to think how brandy lies!

OLIVER WENDELL HOLMES, SR.

No nation is drunken where wine is cheap; and none sober where the dearness of wine substitutes ardent spirits as the common beverage. It is, in truth, the only antidote to the bane of whiskey.

THOMAS JEFFERSON, IN A LETTER TO
M. DE NEUVILLE, DECEMBER 12, 1818

Wine: An infallible antidote to commonsense and seriousness; and excuse for deeds otherwise unforgivable.

ELBERT HUBBARD, THE ROYCROFT DICTIONARY AND
BOOK OF EPIGRAMS

One of the oldest and quietest roads to content-
ment lies through the conventional trinity of wine,
woman and song.

REXFORD GUY TUGWELL, IN A SPEECH AT THE WOMEN'S
NATIONAL DEMOCRATIC CLUB, WASHINGTON, DC, MAY 1934

Wine, wit and wisdom.
Wine enough to sharpen wit,
Wit enough to give zest to wine,
Wisdom enough to "shut down" at the right time.

ANONYMOUS

'Tis a pity wine should be so deleterious,
For tea and coffee leave us much more serious.

LORD BYRON

———•◦•◦•———

The flavor of wine is like delicate poetry.

LOUIS PASTEUR

Wedlock's like wine—not properly judged of till the second glass.

ERNEST JARROLD

One of the disadvantages of wine is that it makes a man mistake words for thoughts.

SAMUEL JOHNSON

Let those who drink not, but austerely dine, dry up in law; the Muses smell of wine.

HORACE

———•·•·•———

A man may surely be allowed to take a glass of wine by his own fireside.

RICHARD BRINSLEY SHERIDAN, SAID WHILE WATCHING HIS THEATRE, THE DRURY LANE, BURN TO THE GROUND

Who loves not woman, wine and song.
Remains a fool his whole life long.

MARTIN LUTHER

———◦•◦———

Let us have wine and women, mirth and laughter,
Sermons and soda-water the day after.

LORD BYRON, *DON JUAN*

Men who have communion in nothing else can sympathetically eat together, can still rise into some glow of brotherhood over food and wine.

THOMAS CARLYLE,
SCOTTISH ESSAYIST AND HISTORIAN

A waltz and a glass of wine can invite an encore.

JOHANN STRAUSS,
AUSTRIAN COMPOSER

I rather like bad wine; one gets so bored with good wine.

BENJAMIN DISRAELI,
BRITISH STATESMAN AND NOVELIST

———•◦•◦•———

Wine is the milk of the gods, milk the drink of the babies, tea the drink of women, and water the drink of beasts.

JOHN STUART BLACKIE,
SCOTTISH SCHOLAR

Grudge myself good wine? As soon grudge my horse corn.

WILLIAM MAKEPEACE THACKERAY,
ENGLISH NOVELIST, ESSAYIST, AND ILLUSTRATOR

———•◦•———

Do you remember any great poet that ever illustrated the higher fields of humanity that did not dignify the use of wine from Homer on down?

JAMES A. MCDOUGALL,
UNITED STATES SENATOR

Better is old wine than new, and old friends like-
wise.

CHARLES KINGSLEY,
ENGLISH AUTHOR

One not only drinks wine, one smells it, observes it,
tastes it, sips it and—one talks about it.

KING EDWARD VII,
ENGLISH MONARCH

Wine, madam, is God's next best gift to man.

AMBROSE BIERCE, *THE DEVIL'S DICTIONARY*

———

In the order named these are the hardest to control:
Wine, Women and Song.

FRANKLIN P. ADAMS, *THE ANCIENT THREE*

There's life and strength on every drop,—thanks-giving to the vine!

ALBERT GORTON GREENE,
BARON'S LAST BANQUET

———————

Champagne with foaming whirls as white as Cleopatra's melted pearls.

LORD BYRON

Champagne is the only wine that leaves a woman beautiful after drinking it.

MADAME DE POMPADOUR

The feeling of friendship is like that of being comfortably filled with roast beef; love is like being enlivened with champagne.

SAMUEL JOHNSON

Meeting Franklin Roosevelt was like opening your first bottle of champagne; knowing him was like drinking it.

SIR WINSTON CHURCHILL

Champagne! In victory one deserves it; in defeat one needs it.

NAPOLEON BONAPARTE

It is my heartfelt wish that it [champagne] spreads joy, peace and happiness.

EMILE MOREAU

———•◦•———

Thanks be to God, since my leaving drinking of wine, I do find myself much better, and do mind my business better, and do spend less money, and less time lost in idle company.

SAMUEL PEPYS

The priest has just baptized you a Christian with water, and I baptize you a Frenchman, darling child, with a dewdrop of champagne on your lips.

PAUL CLAUDEL

We may lay in a stock of pleasures, as we would lay in a stock of wine; but if we defer tasting them too long, we shall find that both are soured by age.

CHARLES CALEB COLTON

Wine gives courage and makes men more apt for passion.

OVID

———•••———

The giving of riches and honors to a wicked man is like giving strong wine to him that hath a fever.

PLUTARCH

A man will be eloquent if you give him good wine.

RALPH WALDO EMERSON

Wine's a traitor not to trust.

ROBERT U. JOHNSON, *HEARTH-SONG*

The unearned increment of my grandfather's Madeira.

JAMES RUSSELL LOWELL, TO JUDGE HOAR,
IN SYMPATHIZING WITH HIM ON HIS
SUFFERING FROM GOUT

Wine has lit up for me the pages of literature, and revealed in life romance lurking in the commonplace. Wine has made me bold but not foolish; has induced me to say silly things but not do them.

DUFF COOPER, *OLD MEN FORGET*

Compromises are for relationships, not wine.

SIR ROBERT SCOTT CAYWOOD

If Claret is the queen of natural wines, Burgundy is the king.

GEORGE SAINTSBURY, *NOTES ON A CELLAR-BOOK*

Penicillin cures, but wine makes people happy.

SIR ALEXANDER FLEMING, ENGLISH BACTERIOLOGIST

It's a naïve domestic Burgundy without any breed-
ing, but I believe you'll be amused by its presump-
tion.

JAMES THURBER, FROM A CARTOON CAPTION IN
THE NEW YORKER

———

[M]any vines growing naturally, which growing up,
tooke hold of the trees as they do in Lombardie,
which if by husbandmen they were dressed in good
order, without all doubt they would yield excellent
wines.

GIOVANNI DA VERRAZZANO, EXPLORER,
UPON PASSING THE COAST OF
NORTH CAROLINA IN 1592

That the wine for export will certainly succeed in Georgia; that himself had made some even of the Wild grape cut down, which had as strong a body as Burgundy, as fine a flavour . . .

AN AMERICAN COLONIST ON THE POSSIBILITIES OF WINE MAKING IN GEORGIA, 1741

The Americans have no liking for wine unless it is sweet.

GUSTAVE KOERNER, UPON BEING OFFERED WINE AT A FARM IN ILLINOIS, 1833

Wine makes daily living easier, less hurried, with fewer tensions and more tolerance.

BENJAMIN FRANKLIN

For when the wine is in, the wit is out.

THOMAS BECON

. . . [W]ine inspires us
And fires us
With courage, love and joy
Women and wine should life employ.
Is there aught else on earth desirous?

> JOHN GAY

I love everything that's old: old friends, old times, old manners, old books, old wines.

OLIVER GOLDSMITH

———— ❖ ————

Bacchus, that first from out the purple grape. Crushed the sweet poison of misused wine.

JOHN MILTON

To happy convents, bosomed deep in vines,
Where slumber abbots, purple as their wines.

ALEXANDER POPE

———⚬⚬⚬———

Pour out the wine without restraint or stay,
Pour not by cups, but by the bellyful,
Pour out to all that wull.

EDMUND SPENSER

Drink to me only with thine eyes,
And I will pledge with mine;
Or leave a kiss but in the cup,
And I'll not look for wine.

BEN JONSON [TO CELIA]

I am not old but mellow like good wine.

STEPHEN PHILLIPS

Wine . . . moderately drunken
It doth quicken a man's wits
It doth comfort the heart.

> ANDREW BOORDE, FROM THE
> DYETARY OF HELTH

———

I am never so successful as when I am a little merry:
let me throw on a bottle of champagne, and I never
lose—at least I never feel my losses, . . . and then,
what man can pretend to be a believer in love, who
is an abjurer of wine?

> RICHARD BRINSLEY SHERIDAN,
> SCHOOL FOR SCANDAL

You needn't tell me that a man who doesn't love oysters and asparagus and good wines has got a soul, or a stomach either. He's simply got the instinct for being unhappy highly developed.

SAKI [H.H. MUNRO]

———

Ordinarily the crushing of the grapes was done by "well-washed Indians," their hair tied up and wearing only a *zapata*, . . . who thrashed about in the mass of fresh grapes until these were sufficiently macerated and . . . fermented into wine in big leather bags.

PHILIP M. WAGNER ON EARLY WINEMAKING
ALONG THE WEST COAST BY THE MISSION FOUNDERS

The discovery of a wine is of greater moment than the discovery of a constellation. The universe is too full of stars.

BENJAMIN FRANKLIN

———◦◦◦———

Wine, one sip of this will bathe the drooping spirits in delight beyond the bliss of dreams. Be wise and taste.

JOHN MILTON

3

Days of Wine and Roses
Proverbs and Prose

God made only water, but man made wine.

VICTOR HUGO, *LES CONTEMPLATIONS*

A drunk should drink his Burgundy . . . in the House of Burgundy.

EDMOND ROSTAND, *CYRANO DE BERGERAC*

Wine is one of the most civilized things in the world and one of the natural things of the world that has been brought to the greatest perfection, and it offers a greater range for enjoyment and appreciation than, possibly, any other purely sensory thing.

ERNEST HEMINGWAY, *DEATH IN THE AFTERNOON*

When I heard that Mr. Sturgis had given up wine, I had the same regret that I had in learning Mr. Bowditch had broken his hip.

RALPH WALDO EMERSON

Wine is bottled poetry.

ROBERT LOUIS STEVENSON

—•◦•—

The dipsomaniac and the abstainer both make the same mistake: they both regard wine as a drug and not as a drink.

G. K. CHESTERTON

—•◦•—

Bronze is the mirror of the form; wine, of the heart.

GREEK PROVERB

Wine poured out is not wine swallowed.

FRENCH PROVERB

———•◦•———

It was a very Corsican wine and you could dilute it by half with water and still receive its message.

ERNEST HEMINGWAY,
A MOVABLE FEAST

Too much talk, too much talk; you couldn't enjoy your wine; you drank a little more than a bottle each. On Wednesday I had nine men to dinner, and they drank three bottles a man; and you'd have heard a pin drop the whole time. That's what I call a pleasant party.

W.R. LeFanu,
Seventy Years of Irish Life

Take counsel in wine, but resolve afterwards in water.

> BENJAMIN FRANKLIN,
> *POOR RICHARD'S ALMANAC*

＊＊＊

Fill every beaker up, my men, pour forth the
    cheering wine:
There's life and strength in every drop—
    thanksgiving to the vine!

> ALBERT GORTON GREENE,
> "THE BARON'S LAST BANQUET"

Women, money and wine have their pleasure and their poison.

FRENCH PROVERB

Of what use is the cup of gold if the wine be sour?

GERMAN PROVERB

The vials of summer never made a man sick, but those which he stored in his cellar. Drink the wines, not of your bottling, but Nature's bottling; not kept in goat-skins or pig-skins, but the skins of a myriad fair berries.

HENRY D. THOREAU, JOURNAL ENTRY, AUGUST 23, 1853

The effervescence of the French wine reveals the true brilliance of the French people.

VOLTAIRE

Champagne for my true friends. True pain for my sham friends.

ANONYMOUS

————•◦•————

Wine can of their wits the wise beguile,
Make the sage frolic, and the serious smile.

HOMER, *THE ODYSSEY*

————•◦•————

Wine makes all sorts of creatures at the table.

AMERICAN PROVERB

Give, in return for an old wine, a new song.

LATIN PROVERB

This wine is too good for toast-drinking, my dear. You don't want to mix emotions up with a wine like that. You lose the taste.

ERNEST HEMINGWAY,
THE SUN ALSO RISES

A bottle of good wine, like a good act, shines ever in the retrospect.

ROBERT LOUIS STEVENSON,
THE SILVERADO SQUATTERS

Lie soft, sleep hard, drink wine, and eat good cheer.

THOMAS MIDDLETON,
A CHASTE MAID IN CHEAPSIDE

I may not here omit those two main plagues and common dotages of human kind, wine and women, which have infatuated and besotted myriads of people; they go commonly together.

ROBERT BURTON,
THE ANATOMY OF MELANCHOLY

Bacchus, that first from out the purple grape
Crush'd the sweet poison of misused wine.

JOHN MILTON, *COMUS*

———●·◦•◦·●———

The smack of California earth shall linger on the
palate of your grandson.

ROBERT LOUIS STEVENSON

———●·◦•◦·●———

Wine is life.

PETRONIUS, ROMAN WRITER

A man cannot make him laugh—but that's no marvel; he drinks no wine.

WILLIAM SHAKESPEARE, *HENRY IV*, PART II

Good wine praises itself.

DUTCH PROVERB

Wine is one thing; drunkenness another.

LATIN PROVERB

For a bad night, a mattress of wine.

SPANISH PROVERB

Wine is a peep-hole on a man.

ALCAEUS

Bring water, bring wine, boy! Bring flowering garlands to me! Yes, bring them, so that I may try about with love.

ANACREON

But nobody in the world, I hazard, knows more about food and drink than this same company, the wine-merchants from the great plains of Burgundy and the Loire, for whom madame composes, like a musician, like a poet, her *coq au vin* in the casse-croute, over against the wine-market.

LOUIS GOLDING

It is better to hide ignorance, but it is hard to do this when we relax over wine.

HERACLITUS

It was a wine jar when the molding began: as the wheel runs round why does it turn out a water pitcher?

HORACE

———•◦•———

One should write not unskillfully in the running hand, be able to sing in a pleasing voice and keep good time to music; and, lastly, a man should not refuse a little wine when it is pressed upon him.

YOSHIDA KENKO

O thou invisible spirit of wine! If thou hast no name to be known by, let us call thee devil!

WILLIAM SHAKESPEARE, *OTHELLO*

You need not hang up the ivy branch over the wine that will sell.

PUBLILIUS SYRUS, MAXIM 968

I intend to die in a tavern; let the wine be placed near my dying mouth, so that when the choirs of angels come, they may say, "God be merciful to this drinker."

WALTER MAP, *DE NUGIS CURIALIUM*

A cocktail is to a glass of wine as rape is to love.

PAUL CLAUDEL

The splendour of the revelries, when butts of wine are drunk off to the lees.

JOHN KEATS

Give me wine to wash me clean
Of the weather-stains of cares.

RALPH WALDO EMERSON,
THE PERSIAN OF HAFIZ

Wine in moderation—not in excess, for that makes men ugly—has a thousand pleasant influences. It brightens the eye, improves the voice, imparts a new vivacity to one's thoughts and conversation.

CHARLES DICKENS

Wine to the poet is a winged steed.

GREEK PROVERB

Bring me flesh and bring me wine,
Bring me pine logs hither.

JOHN MASON NEALE,
ENGLISH HYMNOLOGIST

Wine opens the heart.
Opens it! It thaws right out.

HERMAN MELVILLE,
AMERICAN NOVELIST

Since in this sphere we have no abiding place,
To be without wine and a lover is a mistake.

OMAR KHAJJAM, *THE RUBA'IYAT*

Try counting bottles
Instead of counting sheep
For the right kind of bottles
Will send you to sleep.

ROSEMARY BAZLEY,
THE *BOTTLE DOGGEREL*

Wine wears no breeches.

FRENCH PROVERB

When you ask a friend to dine,
Give him your best wine!
When you ask two,
The second best will do!

HENRY WADSWORTH LONGFELLOW

———•••———

It is well to remember that there are five reasons for drinking: the arrival of a friend; one's present or future thirst; the excellence of the wine; or any other reason.

LATIN PROVERB

The best use of bad wine is to drive away poor relations.

FRENCH PROVERB

Dead lucre: burnt ambition: wine is best.

HILAIRE BELLOC,
"A HEROIC POEM IN PRAISE OF WINE"

Burgundy for kings, champagne for duchesses, claret for gentlemen.

FRENCH PROVERB

Sweet's the wine; but sour's the payment.

CANADIAN PROVERB

Give of your wine to others,
Take of their wine to you.
Toast to life, and be toasted awhile,
That, and the cask is through.

JAMES MONROE MCLEAN,
THE BOOK OF WINE

Thy sacred emblems to partake—
Thy consecrated bread to take
And thine immortal wine!

EMILY DICKINSON, POET

———

I drank at every vine.
    The last was like the first.
I came upon no wine.
    So wonderful as thirst

EDNA ST. VINCENT MILLAY, *FEAST*

A peak in the goblet, reflects a joyful face,
Alone I smile and then drink myself.

> LI BO, *ON THE NINTH*

Four fresh-opened oysters,
Soft as grey velvet,
Cold as—deep-sea water;
One long-stemmed glass
Half full of light Rhinewine,
Tasting of fruit-flowers.

> TREVOR BLAKEMORE, *AN AUTUMN DINNER*

The study of astronomy is wonderfully facilitated by wine.

HERMAN MELVILLE

Wine has drowned more men than the sea.

LATIN PROVERB

The sweetest wine makes the sharpest vinegar.

AMERICAN PROVERB

They are not long, the days of wine and roses.

ERNEST DOWSON, "VITAE SUMMA BREVIS"

Now and then it is a joy to have one's table red with wine and roses.

OSCAR WILDE, IRISH POET AND DRAMATIST

And Noah he often said to his wife when he sat
    down to dine,
"I don't care where the water goes if it doesn't get
    into the wine."

G.K. CHESTERTON, ENGLISH CRITIC, NOVELIST, AND POET

One barrel of wine can work more miracles than a church full of saints.

ITALIAN PROVERB

———

Wine and wenches empty men's purses.

ENGLISH PROVERB

———

Rhineland is wineland.

GERMAN PROVERB

Drink wine in winter for cold, and in summer for heat.

H.G. BOHN

———•••••———

Since the wine is drawn it must be drunk.

FRENCH PROVERB

———•••••———

Wine does but draw forth a man's natural qualities.

RICHARD BRINSLEY SHERIDAN,
THE SCHOOL FOR SCANDAL

You're walking by the tomb of Battiades,
Who knew well how to write poetry, and enjoy
Laughter at the right moment, over the wine.

CALLIMACHUS

Where there is no wine there is no love.

GREEK PROVERB

To treat a poor wretch with a bottle of Burgundy,
and fill his snuffbox, is like giving a pair of laced ruf-
fles to a man that has never a shirt on his back.

THOMAS (TOM) BROWN, *LACONICS*

Wine carries no rudder.

LATIN PROVERB

Wine on beer brings good cheer; beer on wine is not so fine.

AMERICAN PROVERB

When night darkens the streets, then wander forth
the sons.
Of Belial, flown with insolence and wine.

JOHN MILTON, *PARADISE LOST*

Some of the most dreadful mischiefs that afflict mankind proceed from wine; it is the cause of disease, quarrels, sedition, idleness, aversion to labor and every species of domestic disorder.

FRANCOIS DE SALIGNAC DE LA MOTHE FENELON,
TELEMAQUE

———————

Souls of Poets dead and gone, . . .
Have ye tippled drink more fine
Than mine host's Canary wine?

JOHN KEATS,
"LINES ON THE MERMAID TOWN"

Upon the first goblet he read this inscription, monkey wine; upon the second, lion wine; upon the third, sheep wine; upon the fourth, swine wine.

VICTOR HUGO,
LES MISERABLES

—•◦•—

I was going home two hours ago, but was met by Mr. Griffith, who has kept me ever since . . . I will come within a pint of wine.

SIR RICHARD STEELE,
LETTERS TO HIS WIFE

The best wine has its lees.

FRENCH PROVERB

———

And we meet, with champagne and a chicken, at last.

LADY MARY WORTLEY MONTAGU,
THE LOVER

———

Woman is the lesser man, and all thy passions,
   match'd with mine,
Are as moonlight unto sunlight, and as water unto
   wine.

LORD ALFRED TENNYSON,
"LOCKSLEY HALL"

. . . Our valley is his golden cup,
And he the wine which over flows
To lift us with him as he goes.

GEORGE MEREDITH, "THE LARK ASCENDING"

I tasted—careless—then—
I did not know the Wine
Came once a World—Did you?

EMILY DICKINSON, NO. 296

Wine is a cunning wrestler: it catches you by the feet.

LATIN PROVERB

The wine of life comes from bottles not battles.

AMERICAN PROVERB

When wine sinks, words swim.

SCOTTISH PROVERB

Let first the onion flourish there,
Rose among roots, the maiden-fair,
Wine-scented and poetic soul
Of the capacious salad bowl.

ROBERT LOUIS STEVENSON, "UNDERWOODS"

To succeed you must add water to your wine, until there is no more wine.

JULES RENARD

———•❖•———

I have drunk your water and wine.
The deaths ye died I have watched beside
And the lives ye led were mine.

RUDYARD KIPLING, "DEPARTMENTAL DITTIES"

Sure there was wine
Before my sighs did dry it; there was corn
Before my tears did drown it; . . .

GEORGE HERBERT, "THE TEMPLE"

Wine comes in at the mouth
And love comes in at the eye;
That's all we shall know for truth . . .

WILLIAM BUTLER YEATS

In water one sees one's own face;
But in wine one beholds the heart of another.

FRENCH PROVERB

A thousand cups of wine do not suffice when true friends meet, but half a sentence is too much when there is no meeting of minds.

CHINESE PROVERB

There can be no bargain without wine.

LATIN PROVERB

To take wine into our mouths is to savor a droplet of the river of human history.

CLIFTON FADIMAN, AMERICAN WRITER AND CRITIC

———

If you see in your wine the reflection of a person not in your range of vision, don't drink it.

CHINESE PROVERB

———

Fish, to taste good, must swim three times: in water, in butter, and in wine.

POLISH PROVERB

Drink a glass of wine after your soup and you steal a ruble from your doctor.

RUSSIAN PROVERB

———

Give me books, fruit, French wine and fine weather and a little music out of doors, played by somebody I do not know.

JOHN KEATS, FROM A LETTER TO FANNY KEATS, AUGUST 29, 1819

———

From wine what sudden friendship springs!

JOHN GAY

Come, come, good wine is a good familiar creature
if it be well used; exclaim no more against it.

WILLIAM SHAKESPEARE, *OTHELLO*

Count not the cups; not therein lies excess
In wine, but in the nature of the drinker.

JAMES MONROE MCLEAN

Boys should abstain from all use of wine until after
their eighteenth year, for it is wrong to add fire to
fire.

PLATO

I'm falser than vows made in wine.

WILLIAM SHAKESPEARE,
As You Like It

Wine in excess keeps neither secrets nor promises.

SPANISH PROVERB

Truth and folly dwell in the wine cask.

DANISH PROVERB

Wine enters the stomach, and business grows ripe in the brain.

CHINESE PROVERB

The cheapness of wine seems to be a cause, not of drunkenness, but of sobriety. . . . in the countries which, either from excessive heat or cold, produce no grapes, and where wine consequently is dear and a rarity, drunkenness is a common vice.

ADAM SMITH,
THE WEALTH OF NATIONS

I took one sip; I closed my eyes, and every beautiful thing that I had ever known crowded into my memory.

MAURICE HEALY,
STAY ME WITH FLAGONS

———•••———

Red with meat, white with fish, except lox or herring. Rosé with any endangered species or an ice cream cone.

RICHARD SMITH, *A GENTLEMAN'S GUIDE*

The wine urges me on, the bewitching wine, which sets even a wise man to singing and to laughing gently and rouses him up to dance and brings forth words which were better unspoken.

HOMER, *THE ODYSSEY*

———

What is better than to sit at the end of the day and drink wine with friends, or substitutes for friends?

JAMES JOYCE

[I]f we sip the wine, we find dreams coming upon
   us
Out of the imminent night.

> D. H. LAWRENCE, "GRAPES"

If you wish to grow thinner, diminish your dinner
And take to light claret instead of pale ale.

> HENRY LEIGH, CAROLS OF COCAYNE

Bacchus opens the gate of the heart.

> LATIN PROVERB

[I]f such small indiscretions standing on the debit column of wine's account were added up, they would amount to nothing in comparison with the vast accumulation on the credit side.

DUFF COOPER, *OLD MEN FORGET*

Wine is the discoverer of secrets.

AMERICAN PROVERB

Wine is a bride who brings a great dowry to the man who woos her persistently and gracefully; she turns her back on a rough approach.

EVELYN WAUGH,
ENGLISH AUTHOR

Do I recall the night we met? . . . You wore a bandeau on your hair and with the coq au vin produced a magnum old and rare of Chambertin . . . I might forget your lovely eyes, but not that meal.

ERIC CHILLMAN,
GOURMET'S LOVE SONG

———

Wine is the milk of old men.

FRENCH PROVERB

———

I drank a bottle of wine for company. It was a Chateau Margaux. It was pleasant to be drinking slowly and to be tasting the wine and to be drinking alone. A bottle of wine was good company.

ERNEST HEMINGWAY,
THE SUN ALSO RISES

4

Turning Water into Wine
Wine, Religion, & Temperance

Wine . . . cheereth God and man.

JUDGES, 9:13

———•<•=•—————

No man also having drunk old wine straightway de-
sireth new: for he saith, the old is better.

LUKE, 5:39

———•<•=•—————

Men are like wine—some turn to vinegar, but the
best improve with age.

POPE JOHN XXIII

The song of songs, which is Solomon's.
Let him kiss me with the kisses of his mouth:
for thy love is better than wine.

> SONG OF SOLOMON
> CHAPTER 1, VERSE 1

———

In vino veritas, say the wise men,—*Truth is in wine.*
Before the days of Noah, then, men, having nothing
but water to drink, could not discover the truth.
Thus they went astray, became abominably wicked,
and were justly exterminated by water, which they
loved to drink.

> BENJAMIN FRANKLIN

He will tether his donkey to a vine, his colt to the choicest branch; he will wash his garments in wine, his robes in the blood of grapes. His eyes will be darker than wine, his teeth whiter than milk.

GENESIS 49:11-12,
WHEN JACOB BLESSES HIS SONS

———◦•◦•◦———

Listen, my son, and be wise, and keep your heart on the right path. Do not join those who drink too much wine or gorge themselves on meat, for drunkards and gluttons become poor, and drowsiness clothes them in rags.

PROVERBS 23:19-21,
ON THE SAYINGS OF THE WISE

Who hath woe? Who hath sorrow? Who hath contentions? Who hath babblings? Who hath wounds without cause? Who hath redness of eyes? They that tarry long at the wine; they that go to seek mixed wine.

PROVERBS 23:29-30

O true believers! Surely wine and gambling and stone pillars and divining arrows are an abomination, of the work of Satan; therefore avoid them, that ye may prosper.

THE QURAN

I hereby solemnly promise, God helping me, to abstain from all distilled, fermented and malt liquors, including wine, beer and cider; and to employ all proper means to discourage the use of, and traffic in the same.

THE PLEDGE OF THE WOMAN'S
CHRISTIAN TEMPERANCE UNION

Wine has been a part of my life for nearly seventy years. As a young girl, during the prohibition, I remember the overpowering smell of home-made wine in my grandparent's kitchen. And when I hid from my grandma when I did something wrong, I was safe hiding under the bed—she wouldn't dare swish the broomstick near the 5-gallon glass bottles of wine.

LUCY FIDUCCIA, WINE LOVER

If God forbade drinking, would He have made wine so good?

CARDINAL RICHELIEU

———•••———

Truly, it is the nectar of the gods. There is no other drink like it known to humanity. Only wine is used in religions as a sacramental drink. In fact, wine is like the incarnation—it is both divine and human.

PAUL TILLICH, THEOLOGIAN

Give beer to those who are perishing, wine to those who are in anguish; let them drink and forget their poverty and remember their misery no more.

PROVERBS 31:6-7,
THE SAYINGS OF KING LEMUEL

⸺◦◦◦◦⸺

Catholic as well as Jewish tradition makes it impossible to establish a community of religious people where wine cannot be obtained. Wine is part of worship, symbol and expression of the human and the divine.

RABBI LEO TRAPP

They will not pour out wine offerings to the Lord, nor will their sacrifices please him.

HOSEA 9:4,
ABOUT PUNISHMENT FOR ISRAEL

———•••———

If a liar and deceiver comes and says, "I will prophesy for your plenty of wine and beer," he would be just the prophet for this people!

MICAH 2:11,
ON FALSE PROPHETS

"This is my blood of the covenant, which is poured out for many," he said them. "I tell you the truth, I will not drink again of the fruit of the vine until that day when I drink it anew in the kingdom of God."

THE LORD'S SUPPER, MARK 14:24-25

When Christ turned water into wine
There were no drys to scold and whine;
Today prohibitors would rail
And send the Son of God to jail.

ANONYMOUS PROHIBITION SONG

Forsake not an old friend; for the new is not comparable to him; a new friend is as new wine; when it is old, thou shalt drink it with pleasure.

ECCLESIASTICS 9:10

Beer is made by men, wine by God!

MARTIN LUTHER

Wine is as good as life to a man, if it be drunk moderately; what is life then to a man that is without wine? For it was made to make men glad. Wine measurably drank, and in season, bringeth gladness of the heart, and cheerfulness of the mind.

ECCLESIASTICS, 31:27-28

———— •••• ————

That inasmuch as any man drinketh wine . . . behold it is not good, neither meet in the sight of your Father, only in assembling yourselves together to offer up your sacraments before him. And, behold, this should be wine, yea, pure wine of the grape of the vine, of your own make.

JOSEPH SMITH, MORMON PROPHET,
THE WORD OF WISDOM

We then partook of some refreshments, and our hearts were made glad with the fruit of the vine. This is according to the pattern set by our Savior Himself, and we feel disposed to patronize all the institutions of Heaven.

JOSEPH SMITH, MORMON PROPHET
AT A DOUBLE WEDDING

———◆•‖•◆———

Like the best wine . . . that goeth down sweetly, causing the lips of those that are asleep to speak.

THE SONG OF SOLOMON, 7:9

There can be no difference between the guilt of one man, who indulges at the festive board or at a fashionable dinner party, in a revel over Madeira or Champaign until Reason is dethroned, and that of another, who sits over his potations in a dram shop, until its considerate and merciful proprietor pitches him into the street.

U.S. ATTORNEY GENERAL BENJAMIN BUTLER, A DEFENDER OF THE SPIRITS-ONLY PROSCRIPTION

They are drunken, but not with wine; they stagger, but not with strong drink.

ISAIAH, 29:9

Give strong drink unto him that is ready to perish, and wine unto those that be of heavy hearts.

PROVERBS, 31:6

———

Water flowed like wine.

WILLIAM M. EVARTS,
DESCRIBING A DINNER AT THE WHITE HOUSE
IN 1877 DURING THE ADMINISTRATION OF
RUTHERFORD B. HAYES, WHOSE WIFE WAS
A PROHIBITIONIST

———

Wine . . . causes the lips of those that are asleep to speak.

OLD TESTAMENT, SONG OF SONGS

Eat thy bread with joy, and drink thy wine with a merry heart.

ECCLESIASTES 9:10

Then the Lord awaked as one out of sleep, and like a mighty man that shouteth by reason of wine. And he smote his enemies in the hinder parts.

PSALMS 78:65

And wine that maketh glad the heart of man, and oil to make his face to shine, and bread which strengtheneth man's heart.

PSALMS 104:15

Wine is a mocker, strong drink is raging.

PROVERBS 20:1

Poetry is devil's wine.

ST. AUGUSTINE

For in the hand of the Lord there is a cup, and the wine is red.

> PSALMS 75:8

Wine drunk at the proper time and in moderation is rejoicing heart and gladness of soul.

> SIRACH 31:27

Although man is already ninety percent water, the Prohibitionists are not yet satisfied.

> JOHN KENDRICK BANGS, HUMORIST

Wine in itself is an excellent thing.

POPE PIUS XII

———•••———

He will bless the fruit of your womb, the crops of your land—your grain, new wine and oil—the calves of your herds and the lambs of your flocks in the land that he swore to your forefathers to give you.

DEUTERONOMY 7:13

He makes grass grow for the cattle, and plants for man to cultivate—bringing forth food from the earth: wine that gladdens the heart of man, oil to make his face shine, and bread that sustains his heart.

PSALM 104:14-15

———•••••———

And of the fruit of palm trees, and of grapes, ye obtain an inebriating liquor, and also good nourishment.

THE QURAN

With the growth of the grape every nation elevates itself to a higher grade of civilization—brutality must vanish, and human nature progresses.

FRIEDRICH MUENCH,
LUTHERAN MINISTER

———•••———

[P]ure wine is fatal to the recovery of the drunkard, because it intoxicates, often forms the appetite for stronger drinks in the temperate, and its use by the rich hinders the poor from uniting with temperance societies . . . wine in this country, is a most vile compound.

FROM AN 1835 EDITION OF THE
TEMPERANCE RECORDER

Wine maketh merry, but money answereth all things.

ECCLESIASTES 10:19

How attractive and beautiful they will be! Grain will make the young men thrive, and new wine the young women.

ZECHARIAH 9:17

Christ made wine . . . miraculously from water. He attached no warning label to that wine.

BROTHER TIMOTHY DENIER, FORMER CELLARMASTER OF
CHRISTIAN BROTHERS' WINERY

In that day the mountains will drip new wine, and the hills will flow with milk; all the ravines of Judah will run with water.

JOEL 3:18

Go, eat your food with gladness, and drink your wine with a joyful heart, for it is now that God favors what you do.

ECCLESIASTES 9:7

Wine is the first weapon that devils use in attacking the young.

ST. JEROME

———

Only wine of all drinks continues to live and grow in the bottle. It is a baby, then it becomes a young adult . . . and slowly it enters old age, and then it dies. Of all drinks, wine alone recapitulates life. This is why wine is a sacrament.

PAUL TILLICH, THEOLOGIAN

Stop drinking only water, and use a little wine because of your stomach and your frequent illnesses.

TIMOTHY 5:23

———•••———

I will bring back my exiled people Israel; they will rebuild the ruined cities and live in them. They will plant vineyards and drink their wine; they will make gardens and eat their fruit.

AMOS 9:14

After mildew, phylloxera, cocktails and Prohibition, wine lovers have a right to expect from the New World some startling boon as compensation.

H. WARNER ALLEN

———•◦•———

A walk through the Italian quarter reveals wine presses drying in the sun in front of many homes. The air is heavy with the pungent odor of fermenting vats in garages. Smiling policemen frequently help shoo away children who use them for improvised rocking horses.

FROM A NEW YORK TIMES REPORTER DURING PROHIBITION, WHEN HOME WINEMAKING DID NOT HAVE TO BE CONCEALED.

Thirteen years of Prohibition resulted in the loss of nearly all winemaking talent.

PETER QUIMME

————————

How much better is thy love than wine!

THE SONG OF SOLOMON, 4:10

Noah, a man of the soil, proceeded to plant a vine-yard. When he drank some of its wine, he became drunk and lay uncovered inside his tent.

GENESIS 9:20-21

———

The good man, Noah, seeing that through this pernicious beverage [water] all his contemporaries had perished, took it in aversion; and to quench his thirst God created the vine, and revealed to him the means of converting its fruit into wine.

ROBERT C. FULLER

The wine had such ill-effects on Noah's health, that it was all he could do to live 950 years.

WILL ROGERS

———•❖•———

Wine is constant proof that God loves us and loves to see us happy.

BENJAMIN FRANKLIN

5

To Your Health
A Toast to Wine

Here's to the man who knows enough
To know he's better without the stuff;
Himself without, the wine within,
So come, me hearties, let's begin.

OMAR KHAYYAM

Two things show little wit,
The full or empty cup;
If full, then empty it;
If empty, fill it up!

KENNETH HARE

Wine and women—May we always have a taste for both.

OLIVER WENDELL HOLMES

A health, O reader, and 'tis our adieu:
Good luck, good health, good fortune wait on you.
Over the wine please note our loving book.

EDITH LEA CHASE & W.E.P. FRENCH,
TOASTS FOR ALL OCCASIONS

Any port in a storm.

THOMAS WHARTON

Comrades, pour the wine tonight
For the parting is with dawn;
Oh, the clinks of cups together,
With the daylight coming on.

RICHARD HOVEY

A warm toast.
Good company.
A fine wine.
May you enjoy all three.

PAUL DICKSON, *TOASTS*

God, in His goodness, sent the grapes
To cheer both great and small;
Little fools will drink too much,
And great fools none at all.

OLIVER HERFORD,
THE DEB'S DICTIONARY

He that drinks is immortal
For wine still supplies
What age wears away;
How can he be dust
That moistens his clay?

      H. PURCELL

———•◦•———

Here's to Water, water divine—
It dews the grapes that give us wine.

      OMAR KHAYYAM

Here's a bumper of wine; fill thine, fill mine:
  Here's a health to old Noah, who planted the vine!

R. H. BARHAM

———

Here's to mine and here's to thine!
Now's the time to clink it!
Here's a flagon of old wine,
And here we are to drink it.

RICHARD HOVEY

Here's to the man
Who owns the land
That bears the grapes
That makes the wine
That tastes as good
As this does.

OMAR KHAYYAM

When I die—the day be far!
Should the potters make a jar
Out of this poor clay of mine,
Let the jar be filled with wine!

OLIVER WENDELL HOLMES

Fill the cup, fill high! fill high!
Nor spare the rosy wine,
If death be in the cup, we'll die—
Such death would be divine.

JAMES RUSSELL LOWELL

He who clinks his cup with mine,
Adds a glory to the wine.

GEORGE STERLING

For all of labors, none transcend
The works that on the brain depend;
Nor could we finish great designs
Without the power of generous wines.

JAMES MONROE MCLEAN

When wine enlivens the heart
May friendship surround the table.

OLIVER WENDELL HOLMES

Drink wine, and live here blitheful while ye may;
The morrow's life too late is,—live today!

PAUL DICKSON,
TOASTS

6

Vintners' Wisdom

A cook who runs out to buy a bottle of cheap wine may spoil several dollars' worth of food and perhaps an hour or more of preparation with a dime's worth of wine.

ALEXIS BESPALOF

A fine wine lasts a long time in your mouth . . . and in your mind.

CHRISTIAN MOUEIX,
DIRECTOR OF CHATEAU PETRUS

Great wine is a work of art. It produces a harmony of pleasing sensations, which appeal directly to the aesthetic sense, and at the same time sharpens the wit, gladdens the heart, and stimulates all that is most generous in human nature.

H. WARNER ALLEN

Wine is the intellectual part of the meal.

ALEXANDER DUMAS

The pleasures of eating and drinking operate on so many levels that hard and fast rules simply make no sense.

Oz Clarke

———⋄⋅⋄⋅⋄———

Pour it and they will come.

Professor Steven Mutkoski, Cornell University's School of Hotel Administration, when asked how he maintains year after year a class size of over 800 students for his Wine and Spirits class

California Chardonnays just get wiped out by garlic, but a simple Trabbiano-based white does just fine. The key for me is to keep the palate alive throughout the meal, and Italian wines do that with my cooking.

STEVE DEPIETRO, OWNER IL CIGNO RESTAURANT

I tend to drink three glasses of wine a day—three glasses of red wine, of course—one in the morning, one at about noon and then in the evening . . . Drink wine, drink champagne!

JEANNE DESCAVES, WINE GROWER AND
GRANDE DAME OF THE BORDEAUX WINE WORLD

Even Cabernet Sauvignon, when it is grown in Tuscany, is really a Tuscan Cabernet. It has its own style.

MARCHESE PIERO ANTINORI,
ITALIAN WINEMAKER

———◦•••◦———

We think wine is a time of joy, and the message is: "Enjoy the wine and be happy."

STEFANO RIZZI,
A WINEMAKER FROM LE PUPILLE'S

Wine is something magic; you're following it through the year.

LAMBERTO FRESCOBALDI,
WINEMAKER

———•◦•———

The richness, the warmness of the color of [Renaissance] painting, this I would like to have in my wine.

LUCA SANJUST,
WINEMAKER FROM PETROLO WINERY

I've had many wines that have been cellared 10, 20 years. The only thing that happens is that they just smooth out; they don't become jewels.

MATT KRAMER, WINE COLLECTOR AND
WINE SPECTATOR COLUMNIST

———•••••———

[W]hen you get right down to it, a big, fat Syrah isn't a whole lot different from a big fat Merlot.

ROD SMITH,
WINE COLUMNIST

Wine is not like a pair of shoes you can sell to another person. At the moment the wine is tasted, the risk is taken. You don't change your mind five minutes later after other people at the table decide they don't like it.

DREW NIEPORENT,
RESTAURATEUR

I have no doubt at all that those who wish to, and have the financial means to do so, will make better Cabernet Sauvignon in the future than has ever been made in the past.

JAMES HALLIDAY

Invariably, a restaurant with a large, pretentious wine list has a large and pretentious staff.

KEVIN BARRON

———•◦•———

Unfortunately, a lot of people taste with their pocket-books.

TIM MONDAVI,
WINE GROWER

———•◦•———

Just thinking of Beaujolais makes my mouth water! It is one of the most succulent, juicy, thirst-quenching, and all-around delicious wines I know.

DANIEL JOHNNES, WINE DIRECTOR & SOMMELIER FOR MONTRACHET

First you must hold your glass to the light and swirl the wine slowly to study its color. Then you bring the glass to your nose to breathe the wine's bouquet. And then, you set your glass down and you talk about it.

CHARLES-MAURICE DE TALLEYRANDE-PERIGORD

Ask a French wine producer in Bordeaux what wine region in the world has the best chance of competing qualitatively with his, and the answer will not be California's Napa Valley, but Spain.

ROBERT M. PARKER,
THE WINE ADVOCATE

You must let wine approach you in its own way and introduce itself; for then you will find that you have entered into its company, and that is why wine is properly called a companion. The most enduring of companions; the most familiar and putting forth excellence of its own.

HILAIRE BELLOC

The soft extractive note of an aged cork being withdrawn has the true sound of man opening his heart.

WILLIAM SAMUEL BENWELL,
JOURNEY TO WINE IN VICTORIA, MELBOURNE

What Freud was to psychoanalysis, I was to wine.

SAM AARON, OWNER,
SHERRY-LEHMAN WINES AND SPIRITS

No government could survive without champagne . . . In the throat of our diplomatic people [it]
is like oil in the wheels of an engine.

JOSEPH DARGENT,
FRENCH VINTNER

I edit out all the bad stuff and deliver the good stuff.
Seventy-five percent of all wine is awful.

PETER MORRELL, VINTNER

———◦◦◦———

Bordeaux calls to mind a distinguished figure in a
frock coat . . . He enters his moderate enthusiasms
in a leather pocketbook, observing the progress of
beauty across his palate like moves in a game of
chess.

FRANK J. PRIAL

The general mode of thinking always leans on the cliché and on the abstract. People do not return to their palates. People are afraid that they do not know how to taste. They prefer to lean on the rules. With rules you don't have to think; you don't have to taste.

RICHARD OLNEY,
WINE AND FOOD WRITER

The tradition of enjoying food and wine together has become so much a part of our daily routine that it is practically involuntary: food on the table, wine in glass. What could be more natural?

LINDA JOHNSON-BELL,
WINE JOURNALIST

In California wine has only been made seriously for about a hundred years, but the progress that has already been made is staggering. Certainly, the future is bright, for the finest oenologists in the world reside there.

HARRY WAUGH

———•◦•———

The drinking of wine is a celebration of life, good food and special company. It's one of the great pleasures of the world, and its enjoyment is enhanced by some knowledge of its varieties, flavors and styles.

KEVIN ZRALY, FOUNDER AND TEACHER AT
WINDOWS ON THE WORLD WINE SCHOOL

Like the perfect wife, Claret looks nice and is nice; natural and wholesome; ever helpful, yet not assertive; dependable always; gracious and gentle, but neither dumb, dull nor monotonous: a rare and real boon and joy.

ANDRÉ SIMON

Wine is often thought of as a sophisticated and intimidating subject, but with the right tools anyone can develop an understanding and appreciation for fine wine.

MARVIN R. SHANKEN,
EDITOR AND PUBLISHER, *WINE SPECTATOR*

Wine is part of our culture, heritage, religion, and family, and it is certainly an essential part of the good life. When the complete record of wine is known, wine can play an integral role in most people's lives and enhance those lives.

ROBERT MONDAVI

———•◦•———

At the first sip a good drinker will recognize the vineyard, at the second the quality, and at the third the year.

ALEXANDER DUMAS

Port is essentially the wine of philosophical contem-plation.

H. WARNER ALLEN

—◆—

Wine remains a simple thing, a marriage of pleasure.

ANDRE TCHELISTCHEFF, AMERICAN WINEMAKER

—◆—

Of all the world's grapes, the Sauvignon Blanc is the leader of the "love it or loathe it" pack.

OZ CLARKE

Excellent wine generates enthusiasm. And whatever you do with enthusiasm is generally successful.

PHILLIPPE DE ROTHSCHILD,
FRENCH VINTNER

—————

To a lover of Chardonnay wines, the grape variety announces itself as unmistakably as the theme of Beethoven's Fifth Symphony. No other white grape has a more complex aroma. No other white wine has a more welcome caress as it lingers on the palate.

ELEANOR MCCREA,
AMERICAN VINTNER

There is no substitute for pulling corks.

ALEXIS LICHINE,
AMERICAN AUTHOR AND WINE CRITIC

Making good wine is a skill, fine wine an art.

ROBERT MONDAVI

Wine is like music—you may not know what is good, but you know what you like!

JUSTIN MEYER,
AMERICAN WINEMAKER

Sometimes you have to stop and sniff the corks!

> ARNA DAN ISACSSON,
> SWEDISH OENOPHILE

Our joy of the world is increased by an understand-ing of the artistic pleasure that a great wine can give, and a great wine cannot be fully appreciated without some knowledge of its composition.

> H. WARNER ALLEN

Come quickly! I am tasting the stars!

> DOM PERIGNON,
> AT HIS FIRST SIP OF CHAMPAGNE

If you compare ours with the best of French wines, we are definitely not there. But if you compare it to the worst of French wines, we are definitely better.

ANONYMOUS VINTNER,
NEAR BANGALORE, INDIA

———•◦•◦•———

France has been oriented to quality wine production for a very long time. They have found every corner that makes serious wine. In Italy, it is still an early development to go into quality wine production, and so we are, in a way, at the beginning of this revolution in wine.

MARCHESE PIERO ANTINORI,
ITALIAN WINEMAKER

Burgundies, on the whole, do not keep nearly so long as Clarets; they have more to give, more bouquet and greater vinosity, at first, but they exhaust themselves and fade away sooner than the less aromatic, more reserved Clarets.

ANDRÉ SIMON

Good French wine should carry the phrase: "Mise en bouteilles au chateau." This assures you that only the owner of the vineyard has had a chance to tamper with the wine.

RICHARD SMITH

. . . the great Rhine wines strike one speechless with amazement at the first glass, but succeeding glasses, which with red wines grow progressively more enthralling, never quite attain the pinnacle of artistic perfection with which the first taste dumbfounds the wine lover.

H. WARNER ALLEN

———•———

The Wines of Bordeaux give tone to the stomach, while leaving the mouth fresh and head clear. More than one invalid abandoned by the doctors has been seen to drink the good old wine of Bordeaux and return to health.

COMMENTS BY MEMBERS OF THE JURY JUDGING BORDEAUX WINES SUBMITTED UNDER THE NEW 1855 CLASSIFICATION AT THE 1855 WORLD'S FAIR IN PARIS

Although it's often described as the grape of the sensualists, owing to its peculiar blend of the earthy and the ethereal, Pinot Noir sometimes seems better suited to the care of psychiatrists than winemakers.

> LETTIE TEAGUE,
> WINE EDITOR, *FOOD & WINE*

———

Red wine without tears.

> OZ CLARKE,
> ABOUT MERLOT

Syrah . . . was one of my first "wine moments." The wine was iridescent blue-purple in color and stained both the glass and one's teeth. Each sip has a hedonistic mouthful of ripe, freshly crushed black raspberries, and I had never before come across a wine that managed to balance power and finesse as gracefully.

TIM GAISER, MASTER SOMMELIER AND
SENIOR WINE MERCHANT AT WINE.COM

———•••———

I love the history and winemaking culture of Australia. Fruit is still crushed in the 19th-century basket press. . . The emphasis is on powerful, full-bodied, and fully extracted fruit that is perfectly integrated with firm tannins and yet manages to remain supple and velvety in the mouth.

BO THOMPSON, WINE MERCHANT

I'd pick a magnum of Veuve Clicquot Grande Dam 1990. It's made from my two favorite grapes, Chardonnay and Pinot Noir. Champagne is always better in a magnum. Le Grande Dam is one of the great wines of the world—served by itself or with lobster, my favorite seafood.

HELEN TURLEY, WINEMAKER, IN ANSWERING *FOOD & WINE* EDITOR'S QUESTION, IF YOU COULD BRING ONE WINE TO A DESERT ISLAND, WHAT WOULD IT BE?

A bottle of Madeira. Preferably a Bual of great, though not extreme, age. You can drink it anytime. It lasts forever in an open bottle. The high acid refreshes you when it's hot; the high alcohol warms you when it's cold.

JANCIS ROBINSON,
BRITISH WINE AUTHORITY

I'd have to have a red and a white wine. What good is a red without a white to precede it? What good is a white without a red to follow it? It's the natural order of things.

KERMIT LYNCH,
WINE MERCHANT

Wine lovers are more than just wine drinkers; an appreciation of fine wine is part of a sophisticated, adventurous approach to life.

MARVIN R. SHANKEN,
EDITOR AND PUBLISHER, *WINE SPECTATOR*

Good wines can not be made from poor grapes.

WILLIAM E. MASSEE

———•◦•———

The appreciation of fine wine cannot be gained from the reading of books about wine, nor the memorizing of vintage dates: the only way is to drink wine, fine wine and a great deal of it, with a due sense of reverence or merely of appreciation.

ANDRÉ SIMON

Index

Melville, Herman, 98, 105
Meredith, Burgess, 6
Meredith, George, 114
Meyer, Justin, 192
Middleton, Thomas, 89
Millay, Edna St. Vincent,
    103
Milton, John, 71, 76, 90,
    110
Mondavi, Robert, 8, 189,
    192
Mondavi, Tim, 181
Montagu, Lady Mary
    Wortley, 113
Moore, Thomas, 38
Moreau, Emile, 60
Morrell, Peter, 185
Moueix, Christian, 173
Muench, Friedrich, 150
Munro, H. H. *See* Saki
Mutkoski, Steven, 175

Neale, John Mason, 98
New York Times, 155
Nieporent, Drew, 180

Olney, Richard, 186
Ovid, 62

Parker, Dorothy, 8
Parker, Robert M., 182
Pasteur, Louis, 34, 48
Peacock, Thomas Love, 15
Pepys, Samuel, 60
Perignon, Dom, 193
Petronius, 90
Phillips, Stephen, 73
Pius XII, Pope, 148
Plato, 42, 121
Pliny the Elder, 34, 45

Plutarch, 62
Polish proverb, 119
Pompadour, Madame de,
    58
Pope, Alexander, 72
Posch, Mary Lou, 10
Prial, Frank J., 185
Prohibition song, 139
proverbs
    American, 87, 105, 110,
        115, 127
    Canadian, 102
    Chinese, 118, 119, 123
    Danish, 122
    Dutch, 91
    English, 107
    French, 82, 85, 99, 101,
        108, 113, 118, 128
    German, 85, 107
    Greek, 81, 97, 109
    Italian, 107
    Latin, 88, 91, 100, 105,
        110, 114, 118, 126
    Polish, 119
    Russian, 120
    Scottish, 115
    Spanish, 92, 122
Publilius Syrus, 95
Purcell, H., 165

Quimme, Peter, 156
Quran (Koran), 134, 149

Ramos, Micheline R., 10
Raphael, Sally Jessy, 24
Renard, Jules, 116
Ricardo, David, 33
Richelieu, Cardinal, 136
Rizzi, Stefano, 177
Robinson, Jancis, 18, 199

Rogers, Will, 158
Rostand, Edmond, 79
Rothschild, Phillippe de,
    191
Russian proverb, 120

Saintsbury, George, 66
St. John, Bill, 11
Saki, 75
Sanjust, Luca, 178
Scottish proverb, 115
Shakespeare, William, 91,
    95, 121, 122
Shanken, Marvin R., 188,
    200
Sheridan, Richard
    Brinsley, 50, 74, 108
Sichel, Allan, 26
Simon, André, 188, 195,
    201
Smith, Adam, 123
Smith, Captain John, 33
Smith, Joseph, 141, 142
Smith, Richard, 124, 195
Smith, Rod, 179
Spanish proverb, 92, 122
Spenser, Edmund, 72
Steele, Sir Richard, 112
Stephenson, Michael
    (with Daniel
    Johnnes), 22
Sterling, George, 169
Stevenson, Robert Louis,
    81, 88, 90, 115
Strauss, Johann, 52

Tabeek, Frances, 23
Talleyrande-Perigord,
    Charles-Maurice de,
    182